SO-DGI-870

A Family in India

This book takes you on a trip to the simple Indian village of Mehendwara. There you will meet the Kaushik family. Sri Chand Kaushik is a farmer and he and his family live in much the same way their forefathers did. Progress is slow in coming to their village, but times are gradually changing and Sri's children will not work on the land. You will discover what their home is like, what they like to eat, and how they spend their time.

A FAMILY IN
INDIA

Peter Otto Jacobsen and
Preben Sejer Kristensen

The Bookwright Press
New York · 1984

Families Around the World

A Family in France
A Family in Holland
A Family in India
A Family in Mexico

First published in the United States in 1984 by
The Bookwright Press, 387 Park Avenue South,
New York, NY 10016

First published in 1984 by
Wayland (Publishers) Limited
49 Lansdowne Place, Hove
East Sussex BN3 1HF, England

© Copyright 1984 Text and photographs
Peter Otto Jacobsen and
Preben Sejer Kristensen
© Copyright 1984 English-language edition
Wayland (Publishers) Limited

ISBN 0–531–03788–6
Library of Congress Catalog Number: 84–70782

Printed in Italy by G. Canale and C.S.p.A., Turin

Contents

Arriving in New Delhi 6

By rickshaw to Mehendwara 10

We meet the Kaushik family 12

Arranged marriages 14

The last farmer 18

Family life 20

The importance of religion 22

Mealtime 26

Facts about India 30

Glossary 31

Index 32

Arriving in New Delhi

We are on board a steam train, traveling through the outskirts of New Delhi, the capital of India. We have come all the way from Bombay on the west coast of this vast country, traveling northeastwards across part of the Indian plateau, and then north through lowland plains. It is getting to the end of the hot season and the countryside is dusty and dry. The coming monsoon, or rainy season, will restore it to lush greenery.

The train is noisy and packed full of passengers, many standing or sitting in the aisles and corridors. Like most foreigners, we traveled first class. Second-class travel means uncomfortable wooden seats and no air-conditioning. India has

The Indian railroad system is still dominated by steam.

the world's fourth largest rail network, and everyone uses it to travel around the country. At every station there are food and drink sellers, offering *chay* (tea), slices of coconut, bananas, and other fruit. On board there are musicians, entertainers, even fortune-tellers, as well as the passengers. The heat is almost unbearable and the atmosphere is noisy, colorful and fascinating. We are overwhelmed by the sights and sounds of this extraordinary land.

The country of India is a huge peninsula projecting south into the Indian Ocean from the continent of Asia. It is bordered by Pakistan to the west, Bangladesh to the east, and Nepal and the

India is 3,287,000 square kilometers (1,268,782 square miles) in area. Its population is second in size only to that of China.

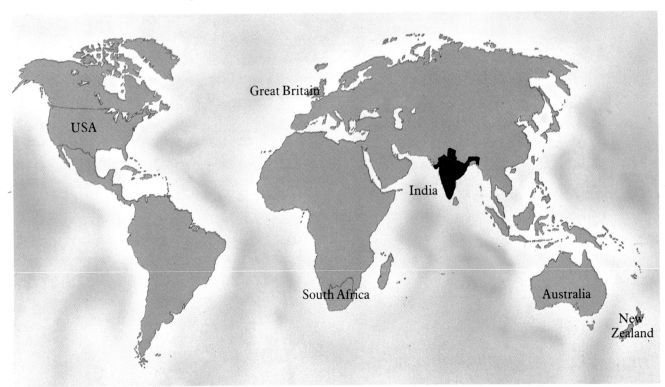

The capital city of New Delhi is unlike any other Indian city.

Himalayas (the world's highest mountain range), to the north. Its huge size means it has a wide variety of climate, scenery, vegetation, people and customs. From the eighteenth century until 1947, India was under British rule. It is now a republic and split into two nations, India and Pakistan.

With much hissing of steam, the train slows to a halt and we have arrived in New Delhi. We've come a long way – Bombay is about 1500 kilometers (930 miles) behind us.

We push our way through the thronging crowds out into the city streets. New Delhi was built in 1912, designed by the British as an imperial capital. It is a city of broad, tree-lined avenues and impressive buildings. New Delhi has a prosperous air, yet India is one of the world's poorest countries, with a population of 700 million. Many of the poorest people flock to the cities to try to find work and as a result the cities often have terrible slum areas, and beggars can be seen on every street corner.

We set off to find transportation that will take us the last part of our journey, to the village of Mehendwara to meet the Kaushik family.

Not far from New Delhi, the Taj Mahal at Agra is a beautiful sight.

By rickshaw to Mehendwara

Above *This street is alive and busy with people and traffic.*

In a side street we find a three-wheeled motor rickshaw and we approach the driver to ask how much he will charge to take us the 50 kilometers (30 miles) to Mehendwara. We haggle and settle on 30 rupees (about $0.90), climb in and set off through the hooting cars, bicycles, rickshaws and pedestrians. Every so often we are slowed down by one of India's sacred white cows, which is either lying down in the road, or making its lei-

surely way across it.

We have left the crowded turmoil of the city behind and are making our way down a dusty road to Mehendwara. Just before we left New Delhi, we stopped and bought some *chapatis* and fruit from a roadside cart. The road is quite busy with buses, carts and people on foot. The heat is tremendous, yet we pass people working hard in the fields – men, women and children.

The little country village of Mehend-

Below *A camel pulling a trailer on the road leading out of New Delhi.*

Above *Children in Mehendwara. Even in the shade the heat is intense.*

wara lies bathing in the sun. The temperature is around 40°C (104°F) in the shade. Goats, black water-buffaloes and holy white cows wander near the houses. Some are mud-built houses with thatched roofs, others are stone-built with tiled roofs.

Our driver halts in the main street, and we are suddenly surrounded by the curious faces of children. We pay the driver, and ask him to return at nightfall to take us back. He agrees, then instructs one of the children to take us to where the Kaushik family live.

Sri Chand Kaushik is waiting to greet us outside the entrance into the courtyard of his house. We shake hands and go inside to meet the rest of the family.

Below *The tiny village of Mehendwara is about 50 kilometers (30 miles) north of New Delhi.*

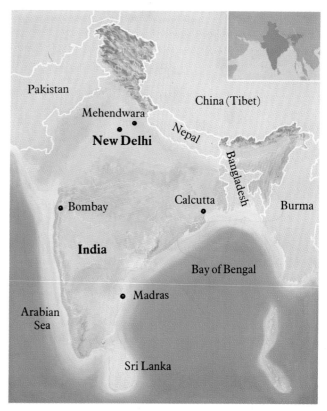

We meet the Kaushik family

Sri Chand Kaushik has lived in the village all his life.

Sri, who is 56 years old, introduces us to his wife, Himatri Devi, and his five children. His two daughters are Geeta, 16, and Saroj, 9, and his sons are Yoginder who is 15, Shiv, 13, and Jugnu, who has just celebrated his sixth birthday.

We sit down in a shady spot in the courtyard. Himatri Devi hands us small glasses of *chay* or tea, drunk with milk and lots of sugar.

Himatri Devi and Geeta are dressed in saris. A sari is a single piece of cloth which is wound round the body, while the loose end covers the head or shoulders. Saris are often very beautiful, in rich colors and, for special occasions, exquisitely embroidered.

Sri tells us about the village. "Altogether there are sixty-four houses in the village," he tells us. "The population is about 500 people. Life does not change here. It was not much different in my grandfather's time.

"However, we are luckier than people in many other villages because three years ago a small hospital was built here. The hospital serves more than twenty nearby villages."

Progress has been slow coming to Mehendwara, but it now has electricity, a nursery school, and there is a school for older children only a short distance away. Most of the people in the village are related, and live more or less like large families. We question Sri about his relatives.

"I have three brothers, who live with their families in the village. My father, Keval Ram, also lives in the village. He is 88 years old and, as his children, my brothers and I have a duty to look after him."

There are no generation gaps in an Indian village, but there are definite rules and traditions which family life must follow. When their father grew too old to work, Sri and his brothers each inherited a house and part of their father's fields. In return, they care for him. Keval Ram spends most of his day on a bed in the shade smoking his hookah.

Keval Ram is now too old to work. His sons make sure he is well fed and cared for.

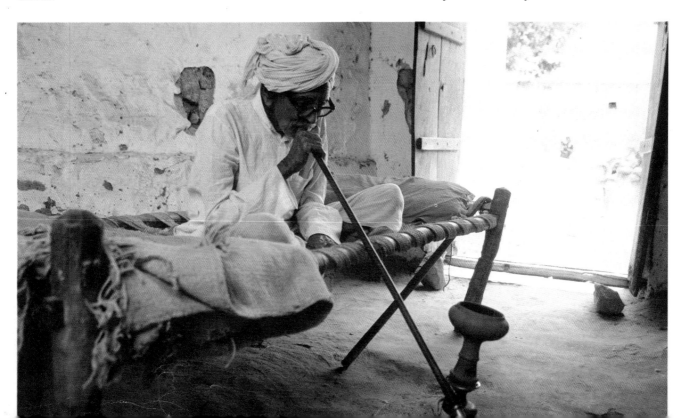

Arranged marriages

A Hindu wedding ceremony. Geeta's wedding day will be the most important day in her life.

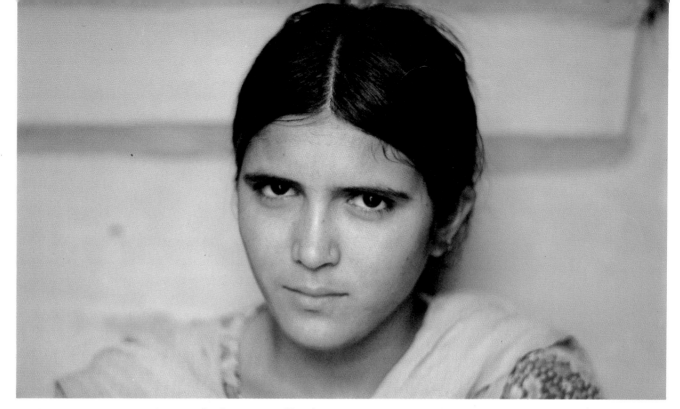

Geeta is sixteen years old and hopes her parents will soon find her a husband.

With the exception of Geeta, all the children go to school. Geeta went to school for five years, but now learns sewing. She is anxious to get married and hopes this will happen in the coming year.

"I am trying to find a husband for Geeta, but it takes a little time to find the right one. He should have a good job or be a businessman, and be at least two or three years older than my daughter," Sri said.

Sri knows that his daughter's wedding will probably cost 20,000 rupees (about $2,000). He doesn't have that much money himself, so it will be necessary for him to borrow.

"To attract the right husband I must be generous with my daughter's dowry, otherwise the bridegroom's parents will not accept the marriage," explains Sri.

15

The women of the village will all help in the preparations for Geeta's wedding feast.

16

Geeta has no influence in the matter of whom she marries and she cannot see her husband before the wedding. They meet and see each other, often for the first time, in the middle of the wedding.

"Who marries whom depends on which parents are able to agree with each other," she explains. "I am happy to accept whoever my parents choose, although it is true that more young people are being allowed to marry for love. I do not know if that is good, though, because there are so many other things to consider."

"Before the agreement is finalised," continues Sri, "I will visit my future son-in-law to see that I can approve of him. Geeta will receive his mother for the same reason. If I think it is necessary I may tell Geeta a little about her future husband."

Geeta tells us about the wedding. "The wedding celebration begins with the arrival of the guests. The actual ceremony may be held that night, or the following morning. Either way, it is the priest's decision. After the wedding, the bridal couple go to stay with the bridegroom's parents and after two weeks, they return to stay with the bride's parents for a time. The wedding is celebrated in both homes with food, gifts, music and dancing."

Sri himself was married at the age of thirty, when Himatri Devi was just sixteen years old. Their marriage was arranged in exactly the same way by their parents, and the wedding followed the same traditions.

A Hindu bride in her wedding dress. Geeta will wear finery like this when she marries.

The last farmer

Oxen are still used by most farmers in India.

About 75 percent of Indians work on the land. Sri sees himself as the last farmer in the family. His father, grandfather and great-grandfather were all born and brought up in Mehendwara and their way of life has changed just as little as the village has changed.

"I get up at 4 am, and by 6 am I'm in the fields where I work until midday. Then I go home to eat lunch and go back to work from 2 until 6 pm," Sri said.

Himatri Devi takes care of all the domestic work such as cleaning, washing and cooking. She is also responsible for the children's upbringing. Together with the oldest boys she also helps in the fields. The girls help their mother in the house, but the boys are not expected to.

"We sow and harvest wheat and corn twice a year," Sri said.

"Apart from these crops, we also grow vegetables and other food so that the family is self-sufficient," he went on.

India is one of the world's leading producers of a number of crops, including tea and rice. Only China grows more rice than India.

The family keeps a cow for milk and at sowing time Sri has to buy two oxen to pull the plow. He sells them when the sowing is over, because it is too expensive just to have them walking around.

"When I come home from working in the field, I eat dinner and relax with a pipe, or sleep. Sometimes I play cards with friends," he told us.

The men of the village relax in the evening after their long day's work.

19

Family life

Sri shows us around his house. It is built of brick with an outside kitchen and washroom. Inside, there is a large bare room with rugs on the floor, but no furniture, apart from beds. We sit down on the floor. We talk to Sri about his children and their future, and Himatri Devi comes and joins us.

"My children shall have an education, so that they can have an occupation. They won't be farmers – there's too little land for that," he told us.

Education is very important in India, and nearly all children go to school, at least for a few years. However, there are still many areas with no schools and many people who cannot read or write.

"The children go to school from 7 am until 1 pm in the summer, and from 9 am until 4 pm in the winter," says Himatri Devi.

With the exception of Geeta, Sri and Himatri Devi hope all the children will attend school for at least ten years.

"The children do about 1½ hours homework each day," says Himatri Devi. "They play a little when there is time, but spend a lot of time helping me in the house, or working out in the fields."

In her spare time Himatri Devi weaves baskets, while Geeta is clever at making decorated head rings for carrying water jugs. Geeta also weaves and sews, and has made a beautiful dress for her little sister.

Himatri Devi and the youngest of her five children, Jugnu.

20

The Kaushik home is very simple. All the cooking is done in the courtyard outside.

The importance of religion

The holy city of Varanasi, on the banks of the sacred River Ganges.

Religion plays a major part in Indian life. About 80 percent of people are Hindus, 11 percent are Moslems, and the rest either Christians, Sikhs, Buddhists or Jainists.

Sri is a faithful Hindu. He believes that what he has, he has received from the gods. In one wall inside his house there is a curtain which can be pulled aside to reveal portraits of the gods Shiva, Krishna, Hanuman, Durga, and Lakshmi. Sri tells us about them.

"Durga and Lakshmi are goddesses. According to the Hindu religion, the goddess Durga created the Earth and Lakshmi is the goddess of plenty. Shiva, the god of destruction, is the most important god, and we pray to him so as not to be destroyed. Krishna and Hanuman represent courage and strength and they protect the faithful from injustice and misfortune.

"My wife, myself and our elder daughter pray together every morning and evening," Sri continued. "It protects us against sickness, harm and a bad harvest. When the other children are old enough,

Sri and his family seated in front of the family shrine.

An ornate statue of Hanuman, god of courage and strength.

they will share in the prayers too," he explained.

Sri also believes in reincarnation. "I have lived in an earlier life, but I cannot remember as what. If I could, then I wouldn't be living here on the Earth now."

We ask Sri what he fears most about his next reincarnation.

"What I fear most is returning as some kind of animal that no one will take care of. But what I become in my next life depends on the good or bad things I do in this life."

Sri believes in reincarnation, and that he and his children will return in new bodies after they die.

In addition to worshipping at home, Hindus worship in sacred temples, and the most devout people often make pilgrimages to holy places. We ask Sri if he has ever been on a pilgrimage.

"When I was young I went with my father to the holy city of Varanasi. It is on the sacred River Ganges and we bathed in its waters to wash away our sins. We also visited many temples and made offerings to the gods."

25

Mealtime

A village stall selling fruit and vegetables.

While we have been talking to Sri and Himatri Devi, Geeta has been busy putting the finishing touches to a special meal of pilaf rice (rice with saffron), dal (lentils), asparagus, mango chutney, chapatis, and halvah (a kind of candy).

All the cooking is done outside, and the family grows most of its own food. Any extras they need can be bought in the village. However, to buy anything special, such as material for Geeta's wedding sari, they have to travel to New Delhi.

Saroj appears with the food arranged on a tray. It looks and smells delicious. Sri encourages us to eat and we do not need much persuasion!

However, many people in India are always hungry. The population is huge and increases at a rate of about a million people a month. We ask Sri what he thinks about population control.

"I think three children per family is enough. We shouldn't have had more, but now it's too late," he said, smiling.

"As for the future, that depends on my children and how good an education they have. I will continue working until I can work no longer, and then it will be up to my children to look after their parents."

"Even if my children move away from the village I know they will come and visit me each week, or at least once a month to make sure I'm well and happy," says Himatri Devi.

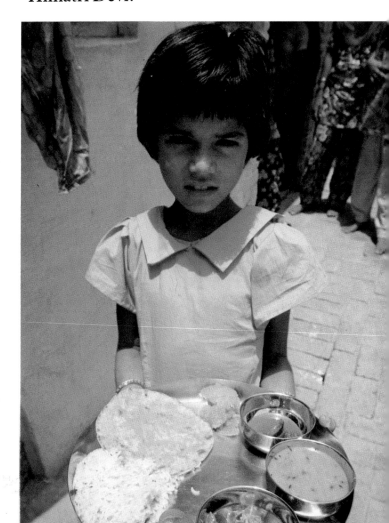

Saroj with our meal. Indian food is hot and spicy.

"They will look after their parents just as I look after my father," says Sri.

It is getting late and the sun is beginning to go down. Little Jugnu comes running in to tell us that our motor-rickshaw is waiting to take us back to New Delhi. Time has passed very quickly and our visit is over.

We rise to go, and the whole family gathers to wish us well and see us off. We have brought some toys for the smaller children, as a parting gift. To our delight, there is a gift for us too and Geeta presents us with a length of silk she has embroidered herself.

The family walks with us to where our rickshaw is waiting, and curious villagers come out of their houses to watch. We say goodbye and climb aboard for the journey back to the city.

Sri and Himatri Devi's children will look after their parents in their old age.

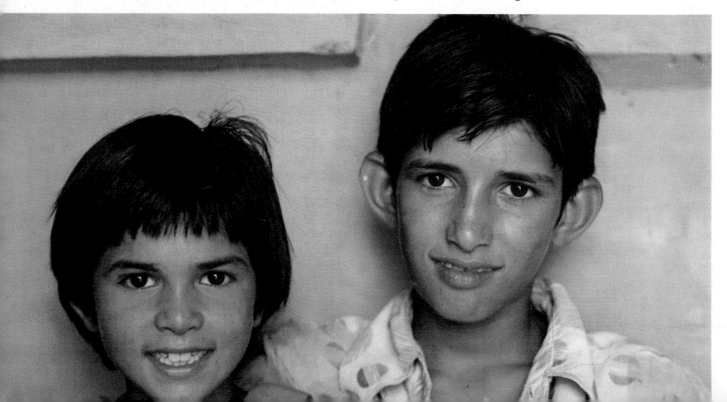

The people of Mehendwara are intrigued to see Europeans in their village.

Facts about India

Size: The area of India is 3,287,000 sq. km. (1,268,782 sq. mi.).

Capital city: The capital of India is New Delhi.

Population: India's population is the second largest in the world at about 700 million.

Language: English is widely spoken, and so is Hindi since about 80 percent of the people are Hindus. There are also about sixteen regional languages.

Money: The currency is in rupees and paises. There are 100 paise to 1 rupee, and this is worth about 9 cents US.

Religion: About 80 percent of the population are Hindus, 11 percent are Moslems, 2 percent are Christians, 2 percent are Sikhs, 0.7 percent are Buddhists, and 0.5 percent Jainists.

Climate: India is vast, and the climate ranges from temperate to tropical. It has three seasons: from October to February cool and dry, from March to May hot and dry, and from June to September the monsoon or wet season.

Government: India is a federal republic. It has a President who is the head of state and elected every five years.

Education: Children go to school between the ages of 6 and 14 years, although this is not compulsory in all areas. At present, children attend school free until they are 11 years old, and in some areas their parents have to pay for their schooling beyond that age. The government aims to make all education free, and to extend it to ten or twelve years in total.

Agriculture: India's chief industry. The main crops produced are cardamom, rice, peanuts, rape seed, mustard, sesame seed, linseed, cotton seed, coffee, sugarcane, jute, tea, natural rubber and livestock.

Industry: India ranks among the top 10 industrial nations. Its industries include heavy engineering, iron and steel production, chemicals and electronics.

Glossary

Chapati A pancake-like kind of bread, made without yeast.

Dowry A payment of money or goods, offered by a bride's family to a suitable husband.

Generation gap The gulf between parents and children in their opinions and beliefs.

Hookah A pipe for smoking tobacco. The smoke is drawn through a long pipe and through a container of water to cool it.

Motor-rickshaw A light, three-wheeled vehicle driven by a motorcycle engine.

Peninsula A piece of land that projects out from the mainland into the sea or a lake.

Pilgrimage A journey made to a holy place for religious reasons.

Reincarnation The rebirth of a person's spirit after death, when it returns to life in another body.

Shrine A place of worship, or an alcove or shelf containing holy pictures or statues.

Temple A building dedicated to the worship of a god or gods.

Index

Bangladesh 7
Bombay 6, 8
British, the 8

Deccan Plateau 6

Farming 19, 30
Food and drink 7, 10, 12, 27

Ganges, River 25

Himalayas 8
Housing 11, 20

Indian Ocean 7

Kaushik family 11, 12, 13, 19,
    20, 23, 27, 28
    Geeta 12, 15, 17, 20, 28
    Himatri Devi 12, 17, 19, 20
    Sri Chand 12, 13, 15, 17, 19,
        23, 25, 27

Leisure 19, 20

Marriage 15, 17
Mehendwara 10, 11, 12, 13, 19

Nepal 7
New Delhi 6, 8, 10, 27

Pakistan 7, 8
Pilgrimage 25
Population 8, 12, 27, 30
Poverty 8, 27

Railroads 6, 7, 8
Reincarnation 25
Religion 23, 25, 30

Schooling 13, 15, 20, 27, 30
Shopping 27

Varanasi 25

Acknowledgements

All the illustrations in this book were supplied by the authors, with the exception of the following: Chris Gibb 8; Alan Hutchison Library 6, 14, 16, 17; John Topham Library 18, 22; Wayland Picture Library 9, 24. The maps on pages 7 and 11 were drawn by Bill Donohoe.